A+
books TM

Eat Your Colors

Yellow Food Fun

by Lisa Bullard

Capstone
press

Mankato, Minnesota

A+ Books are published by Capstone Press,
151 Good Counsel Drive, P.O. Box 669, Mankato, Minnesota 56002.
www.capstonepress.com

1 2 3 4 5 6 11 10 09 08 07 06

Library of Congress Cataloging-in-Publication Data
Bullard, Lisa.
    Yellow food fun / Lisa Bullard.
        p. cm.— (A+ books. Eat your colors)
    Includes bibliographical references and index.
    ISBN-13: 978-0-7368-5385-9 (hardcover)
    ISBN-10: 0-7368-5385-5 (hardcover)
    1. Food—Juvenile literature. 2. Yellow—Juvenile literature. I. Title. II. Series.

TX355.B928858 2006
641.5—dc22   2005027931

Summary: Brief text and colorful photos describe common foods that are the color yellow.

Credits

Erika L. Shores, editor; Kia Adams, designer; Kelly Garvin, photo researcher

Photo Credits

Capstone Press/Karon Dubke, all

Note to Parents, Teachers, and Librarians

This Eat Your Colors book uses full-color photographs and a nonfiction format to introduce children to the color yellow. *Yellow Food Fun* is designed to be read aloud to a pre-reader or to be read independently by an early reader. Photographs help listeners and early readers understand the text and concepts discussed. The book encourages further learning by including the following sections: Recipe, Glossary, Read More, Internet Sites, and Index. Early readers may need assistance using these features.

3 1558 00226 5429

Table of Contents

Yellow Food Fun

Tangy, gooey, fruity, and juicy. Yellow foods have many flavors. But all are the color of sunshine.

It can be sweet, hot, spicy, or tangy. Not all yellow mustards taste alike.

Wiggly lemon gelatin is
the superstar of yellow
treats. This sweet treat
jiggles in your mouth.

Yellow Summer Foods

Ears of corn have rows
of tiny kernels. Use
two hands to eat this
yellow vegetable.

By themselves, yellow lemons are oh, so sour. But mix lemon juice with sugar and water and you get lemonade.

Soft Yellow Foods

Deviled eggs have tasty yellow centers. Mayonnaise and mustard are mixed with the yolk of these hard boiled eggs.

Bananas start out green.
When the peel turns
bright yellow, the soft
fruit inside is ready to eat.

Some potatoes are brown on the outside and white on the inside. But cut and cooked, they become golden yellow french fries.

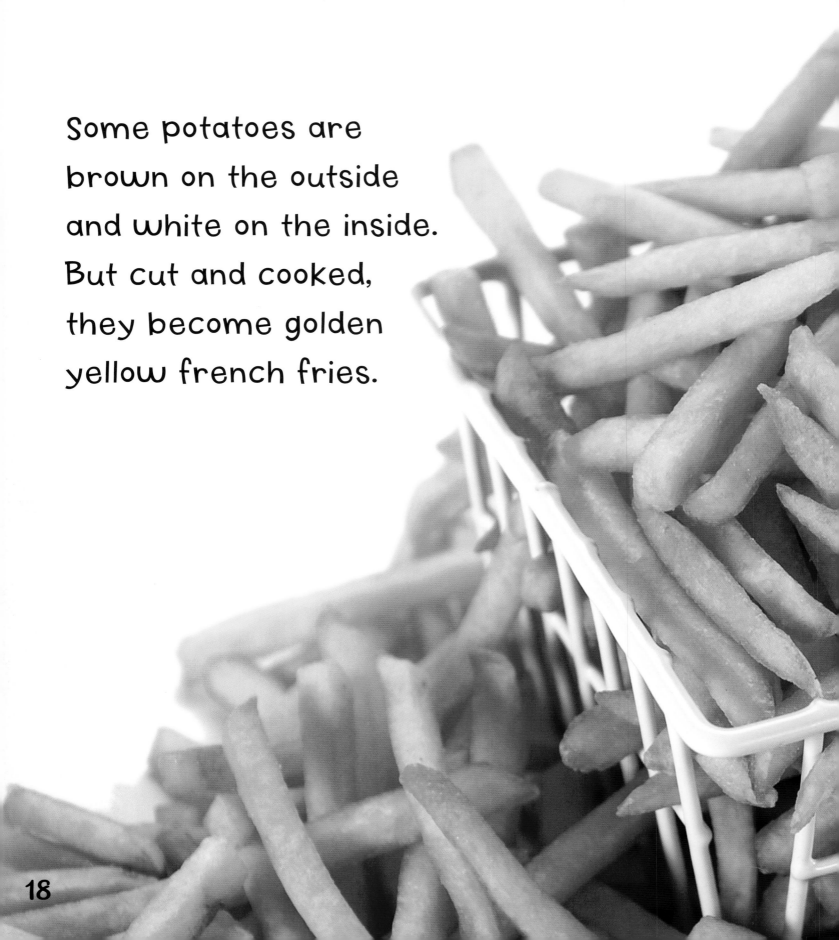

Little pats of soft yellow
butter makes toast
taste better.

Sweet Yellow Foods

Pineapples don't smell
like pine trees or taste like
apples. But this tropical
yellow fruit packs a punch
of sweet flavor.

Thick and sticky, yellow honey is one of nature's sweetest treats. Busy bees turn flower nectar into honey.

Smiling yellow cupcakes look ready for a party. Oops! Looks like someone couldn't wait to taste this sweet yellow treat.

Caterpillar Kabobs

You can bring these fruity bugs along on your next picnic!

What You Will Need

Pineapple
Banana
Wooden skewer
Chocolate chips

chocolate chips

1 banana

1 cup (240mL) pineapple chunks

How to Make a Caterpillar Kabob

1. Ask an adult to help you slice the banana and cut the pineapple into chunks.

2. Put the skewer through the middle of the circle of a banana slice. Be careful of the sharp wooden points. Move the banana piece almost all the way to one end of the stick.

3. Add a pineapple chunk, sliding it close to the banana slice.

4. Add another banana slice next to the pineapple chunk.

5. Continue adding slices and chunks, alternating banana and pineapple, until the skewer is full.

6. The banana slice on the end of your stick is the caterpillar's face.

7. Carefully press two chocolate chips into the banana face to make your caterpillar's eyes.

Glossary

mayonnaise (MAY-uh-naze)—a creamy sauce made from egg yolks, oil, and vinegar or lemon juice

nectar (NEK-tur)—a sweet liquid that bees collect from flowers

peel (PEEL)—the tough outer skin of a fruit

tropical (TROP-uh-kuhl)—having to do with an area of the world that is warm and wet

vegetable (VEJ-tuh-buhl)—the part of a plant that people eat

Read More

Schuette, Sarah L. *Yellow*. Colors. Mankato, Minn.: Capstone Press, 2003.

Whitehouse, Patricia. *Yellow Foods*. The Colors We Eat. Chicago: Heinemann, 2002.

Internet Sites

FactHound offers a safe, fun way to find Internet sites related to this book. All of the sites on FactHound have been researched by our staff.

Here's how:

1. Visit *www.facthound.com*

2. Type in this special code **0736853855** for age-appropriate sites. Or enter a search word related to this book for a more general search.

3. Click on the **Fetch It** button.

FactHound will fetch the best sites for you!

Index

I Want One Too!

Brenda Ehrmantraut
3-4-2008

By Brenda Ehrmantraut

Illustrated By Robbie Short

Library of Congress Control Number 2003092475

International Standard Book Number
Paperback: 0-9729833-0-9
Hardcover: 0-9729833-1-7

First Printing 2003

Published by
Bubble Gum Press
416 4th Street Southwest Jamestown, North Dakota 58401
TO ORDER ADDITIONAL COPIES OF THIS BOOK
contact us at (701) 252-9250
visit us at <http://www.bubblegumpress.net

Illustration and Design
© Copyright 2003 by Robbie Short - All rights reserved
on the web at robbieshort.com

D e d i c a t i o n

For Berk and Marin

XOXOXOXO

B.E.

For Debbie, Matt & Andrew

with love

R.S.

William was six and Megan was three.
Whatever Will had, Megan always said, "Me!"

When Will ordered ice cream, "Chocolate, two scoops."
Megan tugged on his shirt and said, "I want that too."

Will's favorite toy in the park was the slide.
Megan followed him up yelling, "I want a ride."

Bath time and snack time. ..

Run, jump or sit.

This copycat sister just wouldn't quit.

It drove Will so crazy
he wanted to scream.
He decided, instead,
to do something mean.

He set up a trap, clever and slick,
to stop his three-year-old shadow – and quick!

"Hey, Megan. I get to have
something you don't.
So beg all you like,
but get it you won't!"

"What is it?" cried Megan. "I want one too."
She scrunched up her face and stamped down her shoe.

William was tricky. His answer was sly,
"I don't think you'd want one of these Meggie-Pie."

"**Y**es I do! Yes I do! Tell me please? Pretty please?"
	She jumped up and down and grabbed 'round his knees.

"**A**lright," sighed William,
"but there's not one for you.
I'm getting a shot tomorrow at two."

She smiled a big smile and ran out for mother.
"I want one too, Mommy, just like my brother."

"Can I have a shot? Can I get one too?
What color is it? Can I get it in blue?"

Mother said, "Hush Megan. Please quiet down."
"But I want one too," Megan said with a frown.

Off to the doctor they went the next day.
And Megan was planning to get her own way!

Mom told the nurse, "William's here for a shot."
"Me too," exclaimed Megan, "The biggest you've got!"

The nurse smiled at Megan but shook her head, "No."

"See." Said William, "I told you so."

While Will got his shot Megan sulked in her chair.
She pouted and mumbled, "This just isn't fair!"

Then the nurse came back and announced, "Good news! It turns out these shots come packaged in twos."

Megan jumped up to follow along.
"I get a shot too!" she exclaimed loud and strong.

The waiting room snickered,
but Meg didn't know.
They all understood
what was coming. "Oh, no!"

She pranced down the hall,
singing, "Me, Me, Me, Me."
Then five seconds later a colossal

The nurse held up prizes
in red, green and blue.
"Here's the kind Will took,
would you like that too?"

Megan shot Will a look meaner than mean.
"If he chooses red, then I will take green!"

Will smiled wide at his own tricky ways.
He was sure he had ended Meg's tag-along days.